Cat Training Is Easy!

Pamela Anne Moore

DEDICATION

Thank you to my loving family, without their never-ending patience and understanding I could never find the time and energy to sit and write. Thank you also to all of the beautiful cats I have had the pleasure to love over the years and to my current darlings, Cotton and Candy, who were the inspiration for this book. And finally, thank you to you, my readers. Without your feedback and encouragement I would probably never set pen to paper again!

Thank You.

Pamela.

Table of Contents

Cat Training Is Easy!

Pamela Anne Moore

Introduction

Cats, like humans, are loving and stubborn creatures. They have distinct personalities, they react to their surroundings, and they need to learn to grow up in their own environment. The relationship between a cat and its owner is a beautiful one, but it is also a relationship that is built on love and patience.

Like many household pets, cats need to be trained. Some cat owners believe they will not, and do not, need a guide for training their cat, but having a reference by your side is always handy. Teaching a cat to use a litter box, to avoid scratching the furniture, or to stop eating the neighbor's plants can be a long and tedious process. By no means is training a cat easy; like raising a child, you will encounter complications. You will get frustrated, and so will your cat; but those moments when you are ready to give up are just bumps in the road.

Cats are instinctive animals, and they will need proper training in order to hone these instincts and domesticate them. This guide will provide all the need-to-know information for new cat owners, and also any experienced owners that may want to freshen up on their training knowledge. Within these pages you will find all of the key information that comes with training a cat.

You will find out about the differences between indoor and outdoor cats, and many of the responsibilities that come with training each kind. For indoor cats, this may include using the litter box and keeping off the important furniture; for outdoor cats, this may include coming to and from the house, meeting with other outside animals, and interacting with your plants, or your neighbor's plants. Many cat owners decide that they want to train their cats on a leash; for anyone who has trained a dog before, a cat on a leash and a dog on a leash are two very different cases. This guide contains sections that include practical tips for all kinds of cat owners, from the first-time owner to the owner who is adopting a rescue cat for the first time.

Also included in this guide are more advanced tips, such as how to respond to your cat's potentially aggressive behavior. More than just learning how to discipline your cat, you will discover how to understand you cat. This is essential for any owner. How can anyone have a relationship with their cat, if they do not understand the animal? Cats are diverse and intelligent creatures, and they will constantly surprise you. Here, you will learn how to understand your cat—and more importantly, why this is crucial for any animal owner.

Let's face it: cats can be destructive. They scratch the furniture, shred the curtains, rip up the carpet, and maybe they even eat your neighbor's garden. If a cat is going to live with you, you will need to let your cat know that none of these behaviors are acceptable, and this requires discipline. There is a wide range of discipline, from passive to authoritative to authoritarian.

No cat owner wants to institute a passive discipline system; this means your cat will do whatever it wants with no regard to you. This creates a distraught power struggle between you and the cat. Remember: cats are independent creatures, and if you want to domesticate them, they need to be trained. This means you need to develop an authoritative discipline system. This means that you reward them when they perform good behavior, and punish them when they perform poor behavior. This guide will stress positive reinforcement, the most successful way to train your cat. You will learn what positive reinforcement means, and how to institute it throughout your daily interactions with your cat. No cat owner wants to use an authoritarian discipline, which includes being aggressive and rude to your cat. This will only anger your cat and make it more averse to good behavior; this guide will explore the dangers of aggressive discipline, and how to avoid it. Finding the middle ground when it comes to discipline is key, and it will lead to a much more peaceful household.

As cats need strict discipline, they also need playtime. Toys and interaction are an integral part of a cat's daily schedule; if they don't have anyone or anything to play with, they may want to take out their energy on your household items. If you have a cat, spend time with him or her! Just as cats need independence, they also need love. Give your cat love, and they will return the favor.

This guide will cover all of the basics and more when it comes to training your cat. In its contents, you will find information regarding kittens, adult cats, new cats, and adopted cats. Your training methods will change depending on what type of cat you have; obviously you might treat kittens differently than adult cats. Kittens, like children, need to learn discipline in their earlier years, so that they do not encounter behavior problems later in life. Adult cats, if you have had them since they were kittens, should maintain their good behavior, but any relapses into poor behavior can be explained by medical problems, environmental problems, or a number of other issues, all of which will be explored in this book.

Training a cat is a big project; it may not *always* be easy. You may get frustrated and angry, but here is the key: patience is a virtue. As with training any animal, or raising a child, things take time. Cats, like humans, need some time to learn and adapt. Love your cat and have patience with it, and you will yield good results. Cats are great companions around the house and will bring you joy. Whether you are just training a cat for the first time, or whether you are revisiting old methods, this guide will be your best friend when it comes to dealing with cats.

Remember, with knowledge, persistence and patience, cat training *is* easy!

Pamela Anne Moore

CAT TRAINING 101

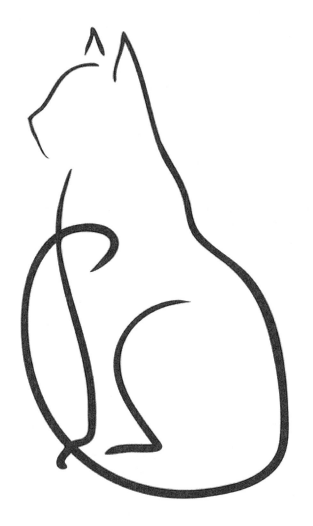

Pamela Anne Moore

Getting Started

Many people wonder if cats can be trained. They are known to be stubborn, independent, and hard to understand. They have the tendency to do what pleases  them rather than what pleases you, and this can cause trouble for the cat owner.

Perseverance is key on your part. Unlike dogs, cats do not usually care to please their owner, and they require more effort to convince them to do what you want. A good first step is trying to understand how they think, so you can adapt. Making them go completely against their natural instincts is not a realistic expectation. However, what you can expect is to instill a sense of both good and wrong behaviors in your cat.

In order to make your cat obedient, there are a few things you have to keep in mind. First of all, remember that cats respond much better to positive reinforcement than punishment. Try to encourage the desired behavior by using affection and rewards. This way, cats will associate good actions with something enjoyable, and their behavior will improve. If you focus on rewarding positive behavior, the cat will stop unwanted, unrewarded behavior. For example, when training your cat for leash walking, praise and give a treat after you put the harness on, instead of punishing your cat when it tries to resist. The cat comes to associate the harness with a pleasant reward and eventually won't resist any more.

Another important thing to keep in mind is not to force behavior. You should not expect cats to perform and enjoy tricks. Be reasonable in both your expectations and approach to training, so you and your cat are comfortable and happy. Focus on behavior cats can handle, rather than trying to teach them new tricks that are unnatural to them.

Expecting a new kitten to immediately adapt to your home is unrealistic. Your home is not yet a natural environment for them, and some adjustment time is needed. They are at an experimental age, and you'll have to keep an eye on them to make sure they don't get into trouble or develop bad habits.

It is up to you to train them for house living, since using the litter box or not chewing plants is not part of their natural instincts. However, kittens are easier to train than adult cats. Their natural curiosity makes them more receptive and eager to learn new things.

It's easier to instill good habits in a cat from the beginning than to get rid of bad old ones. Kittens are still developing and growing, so they have yet to learn negative behaviors. For example, they do not usually fear other pets. So, they tend to show more acceptance than adult cats, which can become aggressive and protective of their territory. Kittens need only a small adjustment period with your other pets, and will be quicker to adapt than adult cats. Kittens are also more open to changes, which makes them receptive to the new things you're trying to teach. They have a lot of energy, won't get easily tired or bored with training, and are eager for new activities. Adult cats lose interest more quickly and would rather take a nap than pay attention to your efforts.

When you are training your kitten to use the litter box, remember to reward them if they have used it correctly. Your praise, as well as rewards, such as tasty treats will make the process a pleasant experience for the kitten. Apply the same procedure in anything you want to teach. Adult cats are harder to convince and require more time and energy for training.

It's in your best interest to start training your cat as early as possible. It will be easier both for you and the young cat. Successful early training leads to a happy, well-behaved adult cat that saves you trouble in the future.

Contrary to what many people believe, cat training is not impossible. Many people have done it, and you can be one of them! Cats can be taught which behaviors are desirable by their owners and which are not. It is up to you to make sure that they put your lessons to good use. Keep in mind that cats are independent animals, and you may have a harder time than training a dog.

There are certain limits to what cats will do, and it is important to understand you cannot override some of their instincts. That being said, a well-behaved cat does not have to act against its instincts; it merely has to show good behavior and avoid undesirable actions. Good behavior becomes part of the routine, and the cat won't feel forced to do something it does not want to do.

First of all, make sure your cat is healthy. If it has hearing problems, any effort to make it respond to your voice is in vain. Physical discomfort can make the cat less responsive and training will not lead to any results. Some physical problems may be the reason your cat is not responsive to your training efforts. For example, bladder problems may cause your cat to eliminate involuntarily all over the house, and any effort on your part to train the cat in correct litter box use may fall flat.

Second, keep in mind that cat training takes a lot of patience. While dogs want to please their owners, cats are independent animals more interested in what pleases them. They don't try to entertain you or make you happy; instead, train them in ways that make sense to them. Using a litter box to eliminate is perfectly fine, but performing tricks is something cats look at with indifference.

Cats respond to positive reinforcement, however. Just because you're rewarding good behavior doesn't mean bad behavior should not also receive an action from you. Make sure you decide on a harmless solution that will also be unpleasant enough to make the cat stop what it's doing. For example, say your cat is chewing on plants. There are several perfectly safe plant sprays you can find at pet shops that act as a cat repellent.

Keep in mind that each cat is different, and some may be easier to train than others. Don't lose patience, and don't worry if training takes longer than you expected. As long as your cat is healthy, keep persisting.

Cat Training Problems

Cat training is not without its problems, especially when you compare it to dog training. Cats are independent and stubborn by nature; convincing them to do what you want will take some extra time and effort on your part. Being aware of the problems that typically arise and the ways to avoid them can make cat training a much quicker and easier process for you.

Cats are curious and playful by nature, and this can work both for and against you. While in a perfect environment, cats can become engaged in what you are trying to teach them, in the most common cases they will quickly be distracted and lose interest in your training activity. To avoid this, try to clear the room of all possible distractions during training; choose a different room than the one where they have their litter box or food bowl, take all the toys and other items that cats may be tempted to play with away and have no other persons or pets in the room. This way the cat can stay focused on the activity you are training it for.

One common problem that arises is when people assume their cats will instantly get along well with children. A cat may sometimes feel threatened if it's over-handled by over-affectionate persons like children. In these cases, the cat may bite or scratch so it is best to get the cat used to your children over time. In the first week, make sure you are always with the children when they are interacting with the cat. Teach them to be gentle and careful in their approach, so the cat does not feel intimidated. Let them take things step by step and the cat will learn how to get along with them over time. It is important not to rush things, so tell your children not to expect the cat to accept any kind of petting until it feels comfortable in their presence.

Another thing that cats need time to adjust to is other pets. Cats are territorial by nature and they may feel threatened by the presence of a new pet. They will see it as a competitor and only over time will they fully accept to share the same home with them.

There are many other common problems but the cause is almost the same: owners rush their cats into doing what they want them to instead of realizing that patience is the key to success. Cats need time to learn and that is something you simply need to adapt to as an owner. We will discuss other common problems throughout our report.

Cat Training Tips

Unlike dogs, cats are not pack animals that view an owner as a master to please. Cats are independent, so they see their owner as their equal or possibly as another cat!

Although your cat doesn't see you as a pack leader, they still recognize you as the one providing food and comfort. You can use that to your advantage. When training cats, make use of food as a reward for good behavior. This way, they associate their actions with something pleasant, and it will become part of their routine long after training ends. When the cat misbehaves, let it know by spraying it with a fine mist of water. Or say "no" in a loud voice and interrupt the bad behavior. When you do this repeatedly, your cat will learn what it is not allowed to do.

There is a limit as to how well a cat behaves. Cats follow their instincts, and it is impossible to completely override them. You can control your cat's behavior to a certain extent, but you must learn to adapt to certain actions that are those natural to a cat.

An important thing to consider when training cats is that you will get better results through rewards than punishments. It is better to encourage cats to behave well than to punish them when they behave badly. Bad behavior should get a quick response, in the form of actions that are unpleasant but harmless to your cat.

One of the best persuasion techniques for your cat is noise aversion. Unwanted behavior generates an unpleasant response from you, and the cat eventually stops. A loud clap or saying "no" in a loud voice can cause a cat to reconsider its actions. The cat then associates unwanted behavior with an unpleasant noise, and it should behave better.

Cats can be moody or stubborn, so it's best to train them when they are the most responsive. Waking up a cat or picking it up from its favorite spot for training will not lead to good results. Most likely, the cat will be more interested in sleeping than paying attention to you.

Avoid training after a cat has just eaten. They will see no reason to cooperate, and the reward-based training cats need becomes less effective. Cats who have just eaten also lose interest and prefer a nap than any demanding activity. A hungry cat will pay attention to you, in the hope that it gets food.

Having more than one cat does not necessarily mean more difficulties for you. In fact, you may even have an easier time with training!

Many cats are happier when they have a playmate. However, bringing a new cat in a house doesn't always create instant results.

The "old" cat may consider your house to be their territory, and they won't be willing to share. It may take a while until your cats are able to get along smoothly.

Soon, the cat will form a bond with the new pet. Your cats will be happier and more responsive to training. They can even follow each other's example when they see rewarded good behavior, which makes them learn quicker.

Cat Training Devices

Cats require considerably more time, effort, and patience invested into their training compared to dogs. While dogs are naturally interested in pleasing their owners, cats need some stimulation and more thought put into the way you are trying to gain their attention. Luckily there are training devices on the market that help you do just that. They are designed to stimulate the cat's instincts in a way that is useful in your training sessions.

One such example of a training device is the scratching box or pole. Cats generally tend to scratch anything they can get their claws on and this can mean some serious damage done to your personal belongings. The furniture, walls, doors and floor are especially prone to cat scratches as there is nothing you can do to let your cat free to roam the house without being able to reach them. Scratching is part of a cat's natural behavior so the best solution is to simply offer them an alternative place to scratch. The scratching post has to be similar in texture to what your cat usually scratches and be positioned near the places that are scratched most often. You can spray the things that you want protected with cat deterrent and move the scratching post just by a little every day, until it is in the location you want it to be.

Another very popular and simple cat training device is the clicker. As the name says, its use is in making a click sound that you can make your cat associate with desired behavior. This goes hand in hand with a reward system: whenever the cat is doing the activity that you want it to, make the clicking sound and then pet it and give it a nice treat. The clicking sounds are always the same so your cat will easily associate them with desired behavior. After a while, when they hear the sound, they will already know what they are supposed to do.

Cat nip or deterrent sprays are also available for you to have some control over the cat's behavior. A cat will become uninterested in places over which cat deterrent is sprayed, while cat nip can be used to attract them to places your cat should be using, such as the special scratching place you have for them. Litters with different textures and scents can also attract cats to use them naturally. After finding the one that your cat seems more comfortable using, then things become much easier in your training.

More advanced devices can be found as well. One example of that would be the self-cleaning litter-boxes. Although they do not do any of the cat training for you, they make the process easier and more convenient. All you have to do with the litter box is replace the waste bags once in a while and you can focus on the training instead of the cleaning. Other devices that make use of technology are sensors that detect when the cat is approaching forbidden areas and react with an unpleasant stimulus that will make the cat go away. They usually use water, noise, or odors that cats do not like. After a while, the cat will learn that those areas should not be explored.

There are various other devices and special toys designed to help you with your cat training process. Look online or at your local pet stores and you will most likely find something very useful for you.

Pamela Anne Moore

BASIC PRACTICAL TIPS

Pamela Anne Moore

Litter Training

You may think training a cat to use the litter box is not hard, as most cat owners are successful.

However, it is not as easy as it seems, and you may find yourself surprised at the trouble you encounter with this simple task. Cats require time and effort investment, which is something a new owner may underestimate. It is better to have a general idea about cat training before you try it for the first time. Then you can be aware of the most common mistakes and try to avoid them. When you start off on the wrong foot, you need to invest more time and effort into fixing what could have been prevented in the first place.

One common mistake owners make is scolding their cat when it eliminates outside of the litter box. Cats can have difficulty linking two different behaviors together, especially when the situation is not as simple as action and reward. In a cat's mind, eliminating wherever it wants is perfectly normal, and your loud voice will not make it realize that this is wrong. Instead, concentrate on rewarding and encouraging positive behavior. Whenever the cat successfully uses the litter box, make sure to reward and praise it.

Cats can also be picky about their relieving place. They don't like to eliminate close to where they or their owners eat, so don't keep the litter box near the kitchen. A private place with little activity is better, since cats like privacy and don't want to be disrupted. Most importantly, keep the litter box clean. The cat should have fresh litter daily, and wash the litter box at least once a week. Cats are sensitive to waste odor, and they will be reluctant to use a dirty box. Cleaning the litter box should become a habit, since training alone is not enough to compensate when your cat is bothered by an unclean environment.

If you're using effective training methods and your cat still doesn't want to use the litter box, then go to a veterinarian. What may first appear to be training mistakes or a stubborn cat can actually be treatable bladder condition, which may affect litter box habits.

Litter training can be a bit of a challenge. But with the right knowledge, it's only a matter of time and patience until you achieve success.

Outdoor Cats

Getting a cat that prefers to roam outdoors to behave properly in your house can be a challenging experience. Even when you provide the cat with  everything it needs, it's not enough to convince it to stay inside. The cat will still try to go outside, to what it considers its natural environment. Cats take time to adapt, and the ones used to living outdoors can become agitated and eager to find a way out. It is up to you to make your home a pleasant living place for the cat.

The first thing is to try and imitate the outdoor environment. You can arrange a nice place for your cat near your largest window. Let them watch nature and bask in the sunshine; it will keep entertained. Eventually they'll become content watching the outside world, without trying to get out.

Make sure your cat has plenty of options for entertainment. This means a lot of toys. Interact with your cat much more often than with an exclusively indoor cat. Provide enough activities so that boredom never becomes a problem. When you two are playing, use only a few of the toys, and keep your play session long enough for the cat to use its energy. Rotate different toys into the playtime, so that the cat doesn't become bored with the same toy. Never forget about affection and positive reinforcement, since outdoor cats typically need more dedication from you, especially in the beginning. Providing them with enough activities helps smooth the transition.

Cat vs. Cat

Cats don't accept changes quickly. This is never more obvious than when you're bringing a new cat into your home. Expecting things to work out by themselves is unrealistic, and you play a big part in how cats interact when they start to live together. Their independent nature can lead to early conflicts, which require your intervention.

As soon as you bring a new cat into your home, the old one will feel threatened. Cats are territorial, and they become aggressive when a "rival" invades their space. In their mind, everything they had access to before now needs to be protected. It takes both adjustment time for the cats and your training dedication before they stop seeing each other as competitors and start getting along.

First thing is that each cat has a safe place to run to. Beginning interactions usually cause both cats to feel threatened one way or the other, so they may display aggressive intentions. Forcing them to stay together in the same place when they're not comfortable will lead you nowhere and make the cats even more stressed. Let them have their own time alone. You are not the one setting the pace. Don't rush the cats into accepting each other, since they both need their own time for that to happen.

During their first interaction, let the old cat slowly approach the new one. If the situation becomes tense for either of the cats, it is better to separate them and wait for another time. Be patient. You can't force cats into getting along. Any attempt to bring them together when they don't feel comfortable with each other's company only creates uncomfortable situations for both of them.

Take into consideration the territorial nature of cats. Make sure they don't have to share things before they accept each other. Provide each cat with its own litter box, toys, and food bowl, as well as its own space. Keep the cats away from each other at first, and bring them together at different times to see how they behave. Keeping each cat's personal belongings separate will help them get over the feeling of rivalry.

Another crucial thing to do is give both cats plenty of attention. Neither of them should feel neglected compared to the other, since that increases the sense of rivalry. Patience is key when helping your cats get along and allow them to interact only under your supervision at first. While it may be a long process, it is possible for your cats to accept each other.

Cat Door Training

When a cat wants to get inside a room, the most common way to announce is meowing and scratching the door until you open it. This can be very annoying and damaging to your doors so you need to train your cat to alert you in a different way. Here are some of the solutions that we recommend.

Cats are curious and playful by nature and you can take advantage of that. One way to do it is putting a bell on string that hangs down from the door. The cat will start playing with the string, thus ringing the bell. This is a good method due to various reasons. The cat will naturally want to play with the bell so you do not need to go through extensive training sessions for that to happen. Secondly, bells are very cheap and can be easily found at numerous stores. There are a few things you need to take into consideration for this solution to work. First, make sure the cat should be able to easily reach the bell, so make sure the string is long enough. A small bell is indicated, as it easier to handle by your feline. In order to attract your cat to the ringing system, you can put a small amount of catnip on the string or bell.

Although cats may naturally start playing with the bell, you will need to train them to associate the ringing with the fact that they will have access past the door afterwards. This is done through the regular reward approach that cat training works best with. In the first few days after hanging the string and the bell down the door of your choice, keep an eye on them to see when they want to come in. Instead of letting them scratch the door and meow, you should encourage them to ring the bell through playing with the string until they do it by themselves. As soon as they do, you need to open the door and allow the cat to come inside where it is rewarded with a treat. Doing so a few times will make the cat learn that the signal which gives access past the door is the bell ringing and your doors will be kept scratch free.

However, there will be times when opening the door for your cat will be bothersome, such as when you are busy or sleeping. The last thing you need in those moments is hearing a constant bell ringing. More than that, there will be times when nobody is home and the cat will become confused when seeing that its signals are not working anymore and may stop using them.

An alternative to strings and bells are the cat doors available on the Internet and in most of the larger pet stores. These are small allow the cat to be able to enter or exit the room whenever it wants, giving it more independence and freeing you of the repetitive task of opening the regular door whenever the cat wants access into a room. Cat doors can be mounted right in your door or on a wall next to it. Make the right measurements for your cat's height and width, as well as those of the door that you want to buy, so you are sure there is enough space for your cat to fit through. Cat doors are perhaps the most worry-free solution for owners once they are installed, as the cat will almost instantly learn how to use them and won't have to rely on you for such a simple task as entering or leaving a room. The only thing which may put you off is the installation, which can actually be done by a specialist if you cannot do it yourself, or the fact that you have to make a hole in your door or wall.

Teaching your cat how to handle doors is essential. Although the ringing bell is a fun method, we would recommend you to give more independence to your cat, as this will also mean fewer worries for you. Something like cat doors are a great solution that lets you sleep or do any other activities, without being bothered by your cat needing to enter or exit a room at that very moment.

Cat Scratching

Cats can have some really destructive behavior, to the point where almost none of your furniture or other reachable personal items are safe.

Scratching is a very natural behavior to a cat and stopping it completely is not something you should expect. Instead, you can aim to have control over where and how they do it, in order to have a happy cat that is allowed to exercise actions which are natural to it, without causing any damage to your belongings.

Cats scratch for a variety of reasons, such as to consume energy, sharpen their claws, mark territories, and many others. The places they choose to do so are basically anything they can reach. This includes walls, furniture, the floor, clothes—the list could go on forever. The key to satisfying the need to scratch and keeping your belongings safe is offering the cat a specific scratching place.

Purchasing or making a scratching area for your pet is the best choice for you and your cat. Pay attention to the types of materials that your cat is scratching and use them in that area.

Once the scratching post is ready, spray the areas of your home that you want scratch-free with cat repellent. You can also place the new post close to where your cat used to scratch before. Whenever it uses the post correctly, make sure to reward it with treats and affection. As with everything, a reward based system works the best. Repeat these actions for a while, until using the designed scratching area becomes a habit for your cat.

After the cat has gotten used to the new post, move it slowly over time to a different location in the house. You need patience as they may immediately revert to their old habits of scratching your belongings if you suddenly move their post somewhere else.

Cat vs. Dog

Cats and dogs are not friends by nature, so expect them to need training before getting along. Your supervision and occasional intervention is crucial during their first moments together. You will need a lot of patience with your pets, since you can't predict how long it takes for them to get used to each other.

Ideally, training should be done as early as possible. Kittens and puppies are much more willing to accept new companions, so expect the adjustment period to be longer if either of your pets is full grown.

Regardless how well your training is, there's only so much you can do. Your cat and dog will need time to adjust to each other. Although you can ease the process, it is not something you can fully control. What you can do is provide a safe environment for both pets to interact under your supervision.

Keep the animals separated at first. Each should have its own food bowl and sleeping place so they don't feel territorial. Be generous with your attention to both animals so neither feels neglected.

When the animals first meet, keep the dog restrained and make sure you have control over the situation. Allow the cat to approach. Don't be surprised if it starts hissing, since that is a natural reaction when it feels threatened. Allow the cat as much observation time as it needs, and don't rush things. It is essential that there is a safe place for the cat to go, in case the dog is perceived as a threat.

Cat and dog training is not easy. It requires patience and understanding, but it can be done successfully.

Cat Leash Training

 If you want to go for walks with your cat, consider that it's not going to be as easy as it would be with a dog. You will need to go through leash training before taking the cat for walk. Cats do not like being restrained by a leash, so even putting it on will take work. There are a few things you need to keep in mind when training your cat for leash walking.

First, be gentle when you put the harness on your cat. As you put it on, have a treat ready that you'll only give out when leash training. Let the cat walk around for a few minutes to get used to the feel of a harness. Repeat the same process for a few minutes per day, for about a week. Then you can attach the leash. It will take some time both for you and the cat to adapt. Remember that cats are not as strong as dogs, so handle the leash gently. It is important to keep this in mind, since failure to do so will cause the cat to hate being in a leash.

Walk at your cat's pace. Dogs and cats are pretty different how they explore the environment. As opposed to dogs, cats need more time to observe and explore an area. Let your cat take its time.

Otherwise, leash walking could become a restrictive experience for your cat, rather than one of exploration.

Don't forget that you also have to adapt. Cats on a leash behave differently than dogs, and you will need patience with them. But it can certainly be done, and it will be worth it when you both go outside and have a nice walk.

Playtime

A cat's playtime is essential to make it consume energy, stay in good shape and let it follow some of their natural instincts. Kittens discover the world through playing and even what may look like innocent interest towards some moving toys is actually them developing or exhibiting their hunting skills. Cat instincts are something that you should not try or expect to change; what you can do is use them to your advantage.

Your cat will be mentally stimulated by playing, since it reduces boredom. A cat that is well entertained is less likely to develop behavioral problems. Cats who lack activities may either try to consume their energy through actions that you will most likely not be happy with or become apathetic. They may also become overweight, which can lead to several serious health problems. House cats are more prone to weight gain due to the restrictions a home puts on their activities and freedom of movement. It is up to you to make up for that through play sessions that will let your cat get some much needed physical exercise. It is one of the most enjoyable ways of interacting with your cat and taking care of its health.

The toys that you choose for your cat should be varied and changed often so the cat doesn't become bored of them. Try some simple toys at first, like stuffed ones or those tied to a string and see how your cat reacts to these. You can quickly get on idea of what your cat is most responsive to and buy something along those lines in the future. Cats can even be entertained by simple moving objects so you can always find something in your house that will get your cat's attention.

When playing with your cat, the idea is to simulate the way typical prey move and sounds. There are even toys aimed to make your mission much easier in that regard. After having the proper toys ready, it very important to let the cat catch them frequently, otherwise it will become demotivating and tedious in no time.

One thing to check when you are buying cat toys is how safe they are. Make sure they are not small enough to be swallowed or fragile enough that it will break into pieces. The fabric used is very important as well, as there is always the risk that your cat will choke with fibers from some of the toys. If you have toys with strings, keep them something unreachable for the cat and only allow the cat to play with them when you can supervise it.

It is good to understand that playing is not just fun but also necessary for your cat's health and well-being. Try to have at least two playing sessions a day, each for 10-15 minutes. It is a great way for your cat to exercise and be entertained. It is good to place these sessions in the morning and in the evening primarily, so the cat uses its energy before you leave for work or go to sleep. It is good for the cat to be able to play alone as well, so leave some toys that are safe to play with unsupervised spread around your home.

Old or overweight cats could very much use some exercise but keep in mind that they will not be as fit as a younger or healthier cat. Try to go at the pace of the cat when using toys and stimulate it progressively until you see some response. Control the intensity of the activity so that your cat does not feel overwhelmed.

Just a few minutes of play every day does great wonders in helping you have a happy and healthy cat. Whether you have a lazy or more energetic cat, they can all be stimulated to exercise using some really common or affordable toys. It is just a matter of time when you will find the best toys and methods to spark the cat's interest.

ADVANCED TECHNIQUES

Pamela Anne Moore

Understanding Your Cat

Before jumping into specific behaviors and the ways to stop or encourage them, it is important to understand your cat. In some instances it may seem as though your furry friend is waging psychological warfare on you and, truth be told, turning the tables and digging into your cat's psyche is a good way to begin to deal with problem behavior. In almost all cases a "bad cat" is simply a misunderstood cat.

The adage goes, "Seek first to understand, then to be understood." This is very applicable to your feline friend. Understanding why your cat acts a certain way will allow you to modify your own behavior to prevent those actions and avoid triggering instinctual behaviors. It will also give you insight when designing rewards for good behavior as well as punishment for bad, though, as you will see, punishment generally doesn't work well with cats (or humans for that matter).

The following rules constitute the basis of cat psychology.

1. Cats do what they want, not what you want

This may seem rather obvious, but there is a subtle message in here that many people miss. You will never force your cat to do what you want. Any attempt to bring about desired behavior through force is guaranteed to backfire. Rather, you must outsmart your cat, in a manner of speaking, by convincing her that she likes a certain activity. This is easier said than done, but this book will offer plenty of tips to help you make this happen.

Honestly, your cat is not trying to control or manipulate you. She is simply trying to convey her wants and needs. If it is necessary or reasonable to meet those needs, then you should do so. This is not a battle of wills, which will quickly turn into a tit-for-tat, but rather a relationship in which you provide for your cat and she provides for you. You will both seek to understand each other and thus build a lasting and significant bond.

2. Cats are curious, but cautious

Cats love to investigate, but they will only do so if they feel safe. Fear is a major motivator for cats and one that will prompt them to behave in ways that are mysterious if not interpreted in the correct light. Cats are more cautious than dogs in most cases. They are not nearly as quick to welcome strangers and, as a result, seem aloof. Really they are just being careful. Mitigating fear and making a cat feel safe can go a long way to helping end or prevent problem behavior.

3. Cats are territorial and hierarchical

Cats may actually be more territorial than dogs and will defend their homes ferociously. Because cats are generally solitary animals, they are more likely to defend a territory and respond aggressively when threatened, particularly by strange animals.

Though they exist in different hierarchies than dogs, cats still respond to authority. They don't recognize the concept of a family (or pack) the way dogs do, so cats are likely to have only one or two companions that they bond with. You want your cat to be your friend, but also to know that you have the final say in what is acceptable behavior. Asserting dominance over a cat has nothing to do with punishment and everything to do with sending the message that certain rules cannot be broken. This is best accomplished through redirection and reward for positive behavior.

4. Cats like routine

Cats are very much creatures of habit. A consistent schedule on your part will help put your cat at ease and reduce the incidence of problem behavior. This is not to say that cats don't like variety, but rather to point out that they need a certain amount of consistency in their home, food, and basic needs.

Moving is a major stress factor in the life of a cat. If you move from one home to another, you will want to take care to spend lots of time with your kitty and welcome her slowly to the new environment. Be prepared for some regression in behavior in this and similar settings, such as biting, inappropriate bathroom habits, etc. Have patience and your kitty will come around quickly; get angry and you will have a disaster on your hands. Establish your old routine in your new home and all will be well.

5. Cats remember

No one knows how "good" a cat's memory is, but he or she will remember acts of kindness and of hostility. A single act of aggression toward a cat can remain with it for a long time, perhaps even forever in extreme cases. Be patient with your kitty at all times. Cats also remember negative interactions with humans and will apply that to all strangers. Even if your cat loves you, she may have been injured by a person in the past, even inadvertently. Take note of such responses to strangers and do what you can to keep your cat at ease.

6. Purring isn't always good

Cats are complicated creatures, much like humans. Sometimes we smile when we are angry, usually right before we explode with anger. Cats really aren't much different. While purring is generally a sign of contentment, it can also signify stress, anxiety, or even illness. Nothing is ever black and white, so learn your cat's shades of grey so that you can better understand how she is feeling.

By the same token, you will note differences in the pitch and tone of the cat's meow. Just like the human voice, this inflection can indicate mood. Paying attention to your cat and its general mood when it is talkative can help you make sense of what these different inflections indicate.

7. Watch the tail

A cat's tail can signify a lot about how it is feeling. In general, when the tail is held high, the cat is happy. A half-raised tail is a sign of distress or displeasure. A twitching tail indicates hunting mode or anger.

8. Cats sleep a lot

Cats sleep to conserve energy. If nothing exciting is going on, your kitty will rest. If you are gone all day and leave your cat without entertainment, you can be certain he or she will be wide awake during the evening hours. You should be prepared for this and play with your cat for at least 30 minutes each evening. This is all the exercise your kitty needs and will lead to a happier, healthy life . . . for both of you.

9. No two cats are the same

Like people, cats have personalities. While there are general trends across breeds, cats are as individual as you and I. Learn to respect your cat's idiosyncrasies the way you would a human partner and you will both enjoy a happier life.

10. Cats are capable of love

Cats are not just binary creatures that act on pure instinct and likes/dislikes. They have moods and feelings that vary throughout each day and throughout their lives. Cats are very capable of love and will reward people who love them with the same affection.

Like humans, cats learn faster and easier when they are young.

You can teach an old cat new tricks, but doing so is more difficult than if you had tried to train your feline when she was a kitten.

For those of you with a kitten, nip problem behavior early before it has time to become habit. Letting your kitten get away with biting and scratching will only confuse it as to why you dislike that behavior when it is older and can cause real damage to your fingers with its teeth. Try to plan ahead with your kitten so as to avoid problems when he or she is older.

Asserting Dominance

Asserting dominance is a common technique for dealing with problem behavior, but it has to be done correctly.

Asserting dominance is usually done by holding the cat firmly so that it cannot leave and telling it no in a firm voice (don't yell).

• After you do this, let the cat go off by its own for a few minutes before trying to engage in whatever was causing the distress in the first place.

• Use this method sparingly and only for severe behavior that warrants a clear message (biting).

Many people advocate turning the cat on its back, which is generally not a good idea. First of all, putting a cat on its back puts your arm in the way of the cat's claws and makes it easier for her to kick with her back legs. Second, and more importantly, this can be very intimidating for the cat and even invoke fear. If you are a true pet lover, you only want your cat to respect you, not fear you.

If your cat is difficult to control, an old blanket or towel can help you keep her contained and avoid her claws. Simply wrap her back legs first and then her front legs so they are contained. Leave her head free. Hold her gently in this position until she stops struggling and then let her go.

Asserting dominance with cats is difficult and will likely take time.

• What is important to remember, however, is that doing it in one setting generally translates to others. In other words, assert your dominance about biting and it will translate to scratching and other behavior.

• Once your cat knows you mean business, she will start to take your verbal commands more seriously.

There is another technique for asserting dominance that often works. Despite the fact that cats tend to be solitary animals, they do not appreciate rejection.

• Even the most aloof cat will want affection from time to time, so you can use this to send a message.

• When your kitty misbehaves, send her to an unoccupied room and leave. In essence, this mild rejection will send the message that what is going on is unacceptable.

This final point is crucial, so don't forget it. After you assert dominance (several minutes after) be sure to pet, love, and snuggle your cat.

Though misguided individuals will tell you this sends mixed messages, it does not. Your cat will learn that you are dominant, but will recognize that you still love it.

You want to send the message that you are asking, not telling, your kitty to behave.

Letting it know you love it after a spat between the two of you is a good way to go about this.

Aggressive Behavior

Biting and scratching are the two most distressing things that your cat can do. Both are painful, both are destructive, and attempting to resolve either can push you to your wits' end. Before you can end either of these behaviors, it is essential that you understand where they are coming from. After all, if a cat is biting out of fear, you will take a very different approach to training than if the cat is biting as a result of overly aggressive play.

Understanding cats is as difficult as understanding humans. Sometimes, even your cat won't know why she is biting, so you will have to figure it out for her. The following are common reasons that cats attack people, including their owners, and what to do about it. Before reading further though, remember that the key to dealing with aggressive behavior is consistency. The more consistent you are in your actions, the easier it will be for your cat to determine what is and is not acceptable behavior.

Annoyance Biting

Annoyance is a common reason for cats to bite or scratch.

• While humans can simply walk away or give a verbal warning to the person who is annoying them, cats are more limited in their expression of irritation.

• As a result of this limitation, a cat will use its claws or teeth to let you know that you are getting on its nerves. Your feline does not wish to cause you serious harm, only to make you understand its displeasure.

You will know that a cat is annoyed based on its posture, the fact that it gets up and moves, and other factors. The action of its tail is an excellent way to determine its mood. Quick, short flicks of the tail are almost a certain sign that your cat is irritated with something. For the most part, the harder your cat's tail is thumping, the more annoyed it is. Try to determine if it is something you are doing.

Body language is important to understanding your cat, but the tail is just the beginning. Ears that are down or folded are a good indication that a kitty is unhappy. Growling and hissing, while not body language, are also good indications that your cat is upset with something.

There are two ways to approach biting or scratching that arises from annoyance. The first thing you should do is seek to understand what is going on that is irritating your cat. They are as particular as we are about being touched, having their belongings moved, or being fed too late. Don't take it as your prerogative to do as you please and think your cat will simply follow suit. They are living creatures like any other and have their own needs and desires. Try to meet their needs the way you would want someone to meet your own.

It isn't always the case that you can alter your behavior to suit your cat. For instance, your cat may find it irritating to have its toenails trimmed, but this is essential for many indoor cats. If she bites or scratches over a behavior that cannot be altered, then you must focus on getting the cat used to that behavior.

The best way to adapt your cat to a behavior is to build up slowly over time. In other words, don't trim all of its nails at once, but rather do one paw and then wait a few minutes or even hours to do the next. When your cat gets through having a whole set of nails trimmed without biting or scratching, reward her in recognition of the progress. You can slowly work your way up, over time, to trimming all of her claws at once. Depending on your cat, this may take days or weeks.

If you do need to reprimand your cat, keep in mind that severe punishment will only make her dislike the activity more. If your cat begins to fear her toenail trimming, then she will start biting as soon as she sees the clippers.

Fear Aggression

Cats are instinctual animals. If you have ever felt the need to run away as the result of a frightening or stressful situation, then you will understand why your cat is biting or scratching when it is afraid. Fear aggression is easy to combat so long as you understand what is creating the fear. Before we go further into this topic, one thing is essential to know about fear biting.

If your cat is aggressive due to fear, punishing her will only make it worse. The last thing you want to do is swat or hit your cat in any circumstance, but especially if it is reacting out of fear. This will reinforce its fear and leave it thinking that you are unwilling to protect it. This is not only a bad situation for the cat, but it will also make your attempts to stop the aggression that much more difficult.

Understanding fear aggression begins with observing body language. A cat that is fearful will have dilated (enlarged) pupils. More importantly, she will raise her hackles, which is to say the fur on her back will stand on end. The fur on her tail will do the same thing. If your cat's tail looks like a Christmas tree, then it is probably afraid.

Finally, a cat that is afraid will have a characteristic posture. It will be low to the ground and its muscles will be tense. It will be facing whatever is causing its fear, but will be "leaning" away from whatever it is. In other words, it is ready to either fight or run.

The best way to combat fear aggression is to remove whatever is frightening your cat. If it is a particular person that your kitty fears, then you will have to slowly expose your cat to that person. The best solution is to do this in a quiet setting that your cat can retreat from at any time. Don't hold your cat, but rather let the person she fears sit with his hand out and give the cat time to come near. The individual should not try to pet the cat too soon, but rather let the kitty sniff and rub for a bit until it calms down. The key is to let the cat come to you. Should the cat attempt to bite or scratch, assert dominance through isolation.

Loving your cat to mitigate fear is a good strategy, but should be done carefully. You don't want your cat to feel trapped and you want to avoid getting clawed or injured because your cat is attempting to run. It is not uncommon for a terrified cat to dig its claws into your flesh as it tries to climb up to your head or over your shoulder to avoid danger. This is not because the cat wants to hurt you, but because it is terrified beyond rational behavior.

If you want to expose your cat to the item or situation it fears while holding it, do so slowly. Wrapping the kitty in an old blanket or towel is a good idea to avoid getting injured. Move slowly toward the feared object and pay close attention to your cat's response. If she appears too fearful, back away. Throughout the process speak in a soft, soothing tone and gently stroke your furry friend to reassure her that you are present. It is a good idea to start using the blanket as a safety item before trying to expose the cat to whatever it fears. This will help it to understand that it is safe and therefore reduce anxiety.

Play Aggression

It is normal for cats to bite one another when they play. Kittens are particularly fond of this kind of play. Your cat may consider you to be just a slightly larger, less hairy cat and play with you the same way she would with any other cat. The best way to end this behavior is to start teaching your cat what is acceptable play at a young age, though older cats can certainly learn.

First of all, never use your bare hand to play with your cat. This sends the message that it is okay for kitty to attack, bite, and scratch humans. The same premise goes for any other part of your body. Send a consistent message to your cat that aggressive play is fine so long as it is with toys and not living things. Some people use a glove to play with their cat, which may be okay. Just be prepared for your cat to attack every time you or someone else puts on gloves.

Kittens are very receptive to feedback about what is appropriate and what is not. They are also easier to handle than adult cats. If your cat engages in play aggression with you or others, don't encourage it. Rather, if the kitten is getting too aggressive during play, simply stop playing. They are usually confused at first, but get the message very quickly. You can include a gentle, verbal

"No" to help your cat become accustomed to this word and integrate it into her understanding of your behavior.

The other techniques to use in this case are dominance assertion and simply walking away. Leaving your cat when its play gets too rough sends the message that you are not having fun. Kitty won't be having fun if you leave either, so she will quickly determine which behaviors are provoking your departure and curb them.

For both older cats and kittens, play aggression can manifest as attacking your feet or biting you in the night while you sleep. The obvious solution to the latter is to remove that cat from the bedroom, but this is not always possible or desired. If you would rather sleep with your furry friend or need to stop it biting your feet as you walk past, then there are a few solutions.

First, tie a bell to the cat's collar. This way you will know where she is and be able to put an end to her play before it gets started. This warning will give you time to prepare so that you can catch the cat and assert dominance or, preferably, redirect its play before it is able to bite your feet.

If the above approach does not work, particularly at night, then a spray bottle may be in order. Cats tend to hate water, particularly when sprayed with it. This technique requires that you stay awake and spray the cat immediately before it attacks you. In general, this should be a last approach because it may make your cat a bit timid. It should absolutely not be used to stop aggressive play behavior when you engage in play with your cat. It should only be used when your cat is attempting to play with you and you are not attempting to play with it.

Two final points about play should be covered.

• First, it is a good idea to keep your cat's claws trimmed, particularly when it is young. This will help prevent damage to your skin and will also allow you to assert dominance over the cat without sustaining injury.

• Second, try to keep playtime consistent. That way, your cat will know when it is okay to go wild and when it is not. A cat with a consistent playtime will make it easier to understand why it should not be biting you at other times.

Other Aggression

The types of aggression covered above are most common, but are by no means the only reasons that a cat may bite or scratch. Other reasons for aggression include redirection, medical problems, and maternal behavior. In all cases, your goal should be to discover the underlying cause of the behavior and attempt to mitigate that problem.

• Medical aggression is usually easy to understand because it happens in an otherwise healthy cat and usually has specific triggers. It may occur when you touch the cat a certain way, during specific times of day, or as a result of exposure to a specific food or chemical. For instance, an older cat that is cranky upon waking may be suffering from arthritis. If your feline friend has a sudden change in mood and behavior, a trip to the vet is in order to rule out potential medical problems.

• Redirected anger means that your cat is attacking you because it is upset with someone or something else. This may be the most difficult behavior to understand and correct because the stimulus could be as simple as seeing another cat outside. The solution to redirected anger begins with patience.

Never get angry at your cat, as that will only increase its aggression.

• You can start off by leaving the cat alone if it is only mildly agitated.

• Put her in a dark room and shut the lights off while she calms down.

If your kitty is highly agitated, then wrap her in a blanket or towel and try to soothe her.

A food treat can be very handy in this particular situation to redirect attention and reestablish trust.

If you think that your cat may be upset about other animals outside, particularly other cats, you can try removing those other animals from the yard or blocking your cat's view. It may also help, if you know the other cat, to introduce the two and let them become friends. Do this only if you know the other cat is safe and free of disease.

Aggression is usually straightforward to deal with and can be corrected with patience, adherence to a standard of behavior, and love.

On very rare occasions a cat will simply be moody. Just like people, the occasional cat comes along that just has temper tantrums. If this is the case and you are determined to keep the kitty around, then you must be extra vigilant about the cat's moods and be prepared to counteract bad behavior by moving the cat to another location until she calms down. In general, these cats should be left alone when they are angry, as this will give them the space they need and send the message that inappropriate anger will result in isolation. This is very much an unusual situation though.

More often than not, aggression can be stopped by understanding why your cat is attacking and getting the message across that it is not okay. Cats are very intelligent, so work with them rather than against them to bring about behavior that you both find acceptable.

Scratching Behavior

Scratching behavior can be incredibly frustrating because it is so destructive. You probably don't want to restrict your cat's movements, but you probably cannot afford to buy new furniture every few months either. The bad news is that scratching cannot be stopped, but the good news is that it can be redirected.

Scratching is normal, instinctive behavior for cats. They do this to maintain the integrity of their claws, to shed nail casings, and to exercise. It is something that cats need to do and, as such, is something that you should encourage in the appropriate context. Cats that cannot scratch will become stressed and frustrated, leading to other bad behavior. You can be sure that your cat will find a place to scratch, so you should make it a place you approve of. Below are some ways in which to redirect scratching to acceptable materials, but first, a word on declawing.

In many countries, declawing a cat is illegal and with good reason. If you are considering having your cat declawed, we hope that you will reconsider after reading this.

The procedure for declawing a cat involves amputation of the first joint of each toe. Imagine if someone was to remove and the tips of your fingers, thumbs, and toes so that you no longer had the final bone that contained the nail. That would be akin to declawing a cat. Not only is the operation itself very painful and the recovery extended, but it can lead to long term problems like arthritis. Additionally, should your cat ever need to defend itself, it will be unable to do so.

Cats derive pleasure from scratching, much as you would derive pleasure from a good dessert, an invigorating run, or a favorite television show. Preventing cats from scratching can actually lead to behavior problems such as inappropriate urination and biting. There are many alternatives to declawing a cat, so if you feel it is your only means of ending scratching behavior, but you care deeply about cats, it is better to find your furry friend a new home. Truth be told, scratching can almost always be redirected to more acceptable materials.

The best way to correct problem scratching is to ensure that it never starts in the first place. Provide an acceptable place for your kitten to scratch and she will gladly do so. Actually, it is a good idea to provide several acceptable places. Your kitten will appreciate the variety and will enjoying having its own spaces for fun and play, which is how they view scratching.

The other key when starting young is to discourage scratching in places that are not appropriate. The earlier your cat learns that some objects are off limits, the more likely it is to make that connection with new furniture, carpet, or wallpaper later. Several of the prevention measures outlined below, such as saran wrap and double-sided tape, work very well for discouraging your kitten from scratching.

The ultimate goal is to redirect scratching behavior because it cannot be stopped altogether. However, redirection will take time and you probably don't want to sacrifice your furniture in the mean time. Thus, you need to take steps to protect your furniture and actively discourage scratching at the same time.

Keep in mind that physical punishment almost never works for cats. They either come to resent you, retaliate, or simply become sneakier about the behavior that you loathe. The goal with a cat is never really to punish because they simply don't understand. The goal is to make the behavior you dislike seem unpleasant to the cat and to make the behavior you do like highly rewarding. With that said, here are some ways to make scratching unpleasant.

Saran wrap or other plastic wraps are usually effective and do not cause damage to delicate fabrics or furniture. By wrapping this several layers thick around the target object, you can ensure that your cat's claws will have difficulty reaching the fabric underneath. Saran wrap works because it prevents the cat from "digging" in and getting a good grip on the fabric. This ruins the fun for the kitty and she will quickly seek another place to scratch.

Saran wrap works best for kittens because they will associate the Saran with the object and find it boring to scratch. Older cats are likely to recognize the new addition and simply return to scratching your furniture once you remove the wrap. This is assuming you don't want your furniture wrapped in plastic for the rest of its days. It is still worth a try with older cats, but be extra vigilant after taking the wrap off to see if the behavior returns.

Cats are not fond of having things stick to them, particularly their paws. To that end, double-sided tape may be your best friend to stop scratching behavior. The stickier, the better, but you don't need to buy premium tape for this task. Any double-sided tape will work. As with saran wrap, this is likely to work best with kittens.

Cats have a sense of smell that is roughly fourteen times greater than that of a human. The citrus smell that you and I love is hated by most cats. Imagine having lemon or orange juice squirted up your nose and that will give you some idea of what a cat feels when it is too close to citrus.

Many people recommend putting an orange or lemon peel next to the object you want the cat to leave alone. This has three drawbacks: it is unsightly, the peel will rot quickly, and the cat will know when it is absent and thus when it can approach the furniture safely.

The better alternative to a peel is a dilute solution of lemon juice that you can spray on the object of interest. Provided this will not damage the material you are trying to protect, this approach can be quite effective. If you can get just a faint whiff of the citrus, then the solution is strong enough. There is no need to spray concentrated lemon juice directly onto your belongings. The upside to this approach is that, if anything, it will make your house smell better and can be applied long term. Citrus spray is also very effective on walls so long as it doesn't fade the paint or wallpaper. The downside is that not all objects can be doused in water and lemon juice, since they will fade or otherwise be damaged.

Cayenne (or any hot) pepper is another possible alternative to citrus. It can be dissolved in water or used as a powder. It works well for deterring pets, but also makes a bit of a mess in its powder form.

Water sprays are effective ways to send the message to your cat that scratching the furniture is unacceptable. Cats are receptive to this kind of feedback, but there are two caveats worth noting. The first is that your cat may learn that it can wait until you leave to scratch. The second caveat is that your cat may come to resent or fear you. This second problem is unlikely, but will depend on the personality of your feline friend. If your cat is timid or prone to giving you the cold shoulder, then water sprays are probably not the way to go.

Redirecting Scratching

Creating a deterrent is only part of the equation. If you don't give your cat an alternative place to scratch, then the behavior will continue and you will be faced with a war of attrition. The goal is to create a safe and pleasant scratching place while making furniture, walls, and other inappropriate objects displeasing to scratch.

Cats vary in their preferences for scratching materials and orientations, meaning you will likely need to provide several different alternatives for them to try. Many cats enjoy cardboard, but they may prefer it to lie horizontally on the floor or to be vertical (hanging from a doorknob or mounted to the wall). Some cats like twine (called sisal) wrapped around a post. The best solution is to purchase several low-cost options to determine what your cat likes before investing in a more expensive tower or scratch pad.

A scratching area that your cat can also climb is especially appealing and rewarding for the kitty. These systems can be a bit costly, but they are orders of magnitude less expensive than new furniture or even reupholstering existing furniture. You can usually find sales on these from time to time, so keep a fund stashed and buy when the time is right. These products should combine scratching, climbing, sleeping, and other play to provide a complete solution for your kitty. Having a place that is just your cat's is often a great way to encourage good behavior, create a safe haven for the kitty, and promote a bond between you and your furry friend.

As a word of caution, avoid providing your cat with scratching surfaces that resemble the furniture or carpet in your house. Your cat may find it confusing if the same carpet that adorns its scratching post is also on your floors, but one is off limits. Give it a scratching surface that is unique.

Location Awareness

Where you put the scratching pad will make a difference in how quickly your cat gets used to it and, ultimately, whether it uses the surface at all. Cats enjoying scratching after they wake up, so putting the scratcher near the cat's bed will help encourage her to use it. Putting the scratcher near a feeding area can also be helpful.

Avoid putting the scratcher near things the cat dislikes or in locations that your kitty rarely frequents. Just because the closet down the hall is convenient for you does not mean it is convenient for kitty. As a cat owner, it is important to learn that working with your cat is the best way for both of you to be happy. Cats, in many cases, are willing to cut off their noses to spite their faces. If you make life difficult for your cat, she will do the same for you.

When you see your cat making a beeline for her (and your) favorite piece of furniture, simply pick her up and put her near her scratcher. If she is actively scratching the furniture, you may want to first punish her (water spray) and then redirect.

Good times to call your cat over to her scratcher are after a nap or after a meal. You can show her what to do by scratching lightly with your own hands. It works best if you scratch in a way such that your cat has to stretch to reach your location. Stretching encourages your kitty to scratch.

The end goal, as said before, is to make scratching the new surface pleasurable. One way to do that is to reward your cat for scratching where she should. This is especially true when she spontaneously uses the new scratching surface. Treats and loving strokes are the best options, but wait until she is done scratching before rewarding her. You don't want to send the message that she should limit her scratching of the appropriate place.

Catnip is a great treat for most cats, especially if it is fresh. The stuff in the pet store is often old, so try organic grocery stores or places that sell herbs. It won't be as expensive as you think because catnip is sold by the pound and, as a leaf, is very light. Spread this on the scratcher to encourage your cat to use it. Valerian is another great alternative that will have your cat using her scratcher in no time.

Keeping your cat's claws trimmed can reduce scratching as well as the damage that it causes. It is important to remove casings when you trim your cat's claws as these cause irritation that will lead your cat to scratch in an effort to shed the casings. Just be careful not to pull too hard as this can be painful. Casings should come off with almost no effort.

You should trim the kitty's claws every week if possible. Make it part of a hygiene routine where you clip her claws, brush her fur, and do anything else that needs to be done. Reward her lavishly after these sessions and they will become a pleasurable time that you each look forward to.

Leash Training

Training your cat to use a leash will be a difficult task. It is difficult not because your cat will dislike it, but rather because your cat will not understand it. Teaching a cat to use a leash takes time, patience, and ingenuity.

If, at any time, your cat rejects what you are doing, just go back to an earlier step in the process outlined below. Do this as many times as necessary and understand that through patience and perseverance, you will eventually get your cat to both accept and enjoy the leash. Once she learns that it offers freedom to explore the world, she will ask to go on walks.

Despite the difficulties, taking your cat outdoors can be very rewarding for you both. Your cat will find it entertaining and so will you. In this era of indoor cats, problems arise with boredom and obesity. Taking your cat for walks can help to reduce both. As an additional bonus, many cats feel more secure when they know what is outside of their windows. In a natural setting, your cat would explore for several blocks around your home to stake out its territory and create a safety perimeter. By walking your cat, you can help it establish this perimeter, which will make it feel safer and more content.

Collars are a bad idea for just about any pet (except maybe lizards) and especially dangerous for cats. The problem with collars is that they put pressure on the neck, throat, and hyoid bone. Repeated stress to the throat can cause it to collapse, leading to breathing problems or even suffocation. For cats, the hyoid bone is particularly fragile and can easily be fractured by a collar.

A harness is a much better option because it distributes pressure evenly across the chest and ribs. Additionally, for cats, the harness will not be a problem should your feline friend happen to break free of your grasp and climb a tree or dart under a bush. Collars can get caught on bushes, trees, and other objects that can trap the cat or, at worst, cause strangulation. This is why cat collars often have breakaway designs. Clearly a breakaway collar won't work for leash training, so just stick with the harness.

Before even attempting to put the harness on your cat, you should let her get accustomed to it and comfortable with touching it. Let her play with it and learn that it is a fun item, not one to be feared.

Once your kitty is used to the harness, try draping it over her to let her get used to how it feels. Don't force this behavior, but incorporate it into play. This will allow your cat become accustomed to having the harness on her without having it restrict her movements. Do this in a safe place and make it fun.

Once your cat is happy with the harness, put it on her in a safe location. You may not get it all the way on the first time, which is fine. Just be patient and eventually the kitty will let you put it on completely. You want your cat to be fully comfortable wearing the harness in normal activities before attempting the leash.

When you do put the harness on, make sure it is fitted well. A harness should be snug, but not tight and should allow free range of all limbs. A harness that is too tight will restrict breathing and may pinch. A harness that is too loose will cause the cat to trip and may lead to injury. The right setting is one in which you can slip a finger between your cat's ribs and the harness.

After letting your cat run around and play in the harness for some time, you are ready to attach the lead. Attach it and let your cat drag it around for some time. This will allow her to get used to the weight and learn that the lead is fun and not intimidating.

Walking

Once your kitty is accustomed to the lead, you are ready to start some actual walking. It is best to start indoors where the environment can be controlled. This is a good time to begin introducing commands as well. Keep them simple and friendly. You want your cat (and yourself) to enjoy this process.

Once kitty is happy and obedient indoors, you are ready to make the move outside. You should start in the back yard or another safe location. The key throughout this all has been to keep progressions simple. Don't rush anything at this point. Let your cat explore carefully, especially if she has never been out of doors before. There is a lot for her to get used to including new sights, new smells, and new sounds. The process should be fun, so remain patient and be prepared to make many trips in and out as your cat slowly gets used to its new world.

When your cat finally starts walking outdoors, remember not to overdo it, especially on pavement. Cats have very sensitive pads on their feet, more so than dogs, so keep an eye on your kitty. In their natural habitat, cats have about a six-block radius that would serve as their natural territory. Your cat will find it "fun" to patrol this space and will likely discover such activity to be stimulating and soothing.

Try to pick a time to walk when crowds are sparse and traffic is at a minimum. Even after years of walking, cats don't appreciate fast-moving cars, loud dogs, or lots of people. Familiarity is important for ensuring your cat feels safe, so introduce new environments, people, and other animals slowly.

There are many distractions outside for your cat, so it is better not to give her too much leash. Doing so will mean your ability to react, should your cat decide to run, will be limited. Also, remember that other animals can spread diseases, so be cautious about whom or what your cat comes into contact with and make certain that she is up-to-date with all vaccines.

Outdoors

Taking a young cat outdoors should be approached with caution. In general, you should keep your young feline indoors for the first three to four months of its life. You also need to remember that kittens are more curious than older cats and also less perceptive of danger. You will need to make sure that there is nothing to harm your cat outside. Things to look for include:

• Nails, glass, and other debris

• Harmful animals, including bees, wasps, and hornets

• Pest control chemicals like slug pellets or garden sprays

• Dangerous plants like cacti

Most importantly, before taking your cat outside, make sure that she knows her name and responds to calls. When an emergency strikes, you want your cat to either run directly to you or recognize your calls and return after prompting. The outdoors is fun, but also dangerous.

Some veterinarians recommend against walking cats, basing this argument on two lines of logic. First, they fear the unknown and worry that a frightened or startled cat is likely to injure itself trying to escape the leash. This is always a concern, but one that can be mitigated by exposing your cat to the outdoors and all that it has to offer slowly. Clearly, some cats are more skittish that others, so you must be the ultimate judge of how well your cat will do out of doors.

It is also wise to keep emergency supplies on hand. A small towel is a good way to restrain your kitty without causing damage to her or yourself. It can be used to protect your cat and as a safe haven. It might be a good idea to get your cat used to the blanket you plan to carry so that it associates it with safety.

The second reason that some veterinarians are against walking cats is that they believe your furry friend will become obsessed with going out and wish to be outside at all times. It is then possible that she will try to dart out any chance she gets or howl at the windows. Like any behavior, your cat can be taught not to do these things. To most cat lovers, this is not reason enough to deprive them entirely of outdoor activity and most who have leash-trained their cats will argue that this fear is unfounded.

You must decide about the individual needs of your pet, but do not be deterred by speculation that your cat will turn into a raving monster if you start taking her for walks. Most cats are very comfortable inside. They enjoy going out, but also enjoy the luxuries of a warm, dry bed that is free of bugs and danger. Cats are a lot like us; they enjoy what nature has to offer, but wouldn't give up their amenities for any reason.

Letting Your Cat Out

There is absolutely no guarantee that if you let your cat out it will stay close to home. Unfortunately, cats cannot be trained to respect boundaries the way dogs can, and though some cats have personality types that keep them within a confined perimeter, many will wander far and wide.

None of this is to say that you should not let your cat outside. It is simply to make you aware of the risks. Letting your cat outside may seem like a fun adventure, but there are dangers to consider. Most experts recommend keeping your cat indoors and taking her out for supervised walks only. If this won't fit your or your cat's lifestyle, then there are some things that you can do that might help keep the kitty close to home. This chapter takes a look at the risks of letting your cat outside, what you can do to mitigate those risks, and ways to ensure that your cat returns home, at least once in a while.

If you do start letting your cat out, morning is the best time. Most people want to let the kitty out at night, but there are problems with such a strategy. First, letting kitty out in the morning means that she will be more visible to people, particularly those in cars. Second, more animals are out at night, which means more opportunity for your cat to meet with injury. Daytime is the best choice for letting the kitty out.

Some cats don't wander far. If you are in this boat, then you are in luck because you can let your cat out without worry. Usually females stay closer to home and males tend to wander. This is natural behavior and though there are always exceptions to the rule, this generally holds.

Males are also more territorial and thus more likely to get into fights with other cats. Cat fights can be vicious and leave your furry friend with some serious injuries. If you are having problems with other cats entering your yard, look to the end of the chapter for tips on keeping unwanted cats away.

There are certain precautions that you should take before letting your cat outdoors or even before letting it venture near open windows unattended. Taking these steps will keep your furry friend healthy and ensure that you form a tight bond.

Disease can be transmitted through open windows if your cat comes face-to-face with a raccoon or other animal through the screen. It is good practice to keep windows closed if you are unable to supervise the kitty, particularly at night. Your cat should have its full course of vaccinations before it goes outside or near the outdoors unsupervised. This means that kittens need to stay indoors for at least three or four months. This same rule applies to older cats that are adopted but have never been vaccinated.

Having your cat spayed or neutered is a good idea unless you plan to breed it. It is really a responsibility to ensure that an outdoor cat is not populating the neighborhood with kittens. If you have a female cat, she'll be having those kittens in your yard, car, garden, or home. If you have a male cat, there is always the risk that an angry neighbor will show up at your door demanding you do something about the kittens. In short, spay or neuter your cat. It not only reduces the risk of pregnancy to zero, it makes males cats less aggressive and prevents your female from attracting males into your yard.

Many people leave food out all day for their indoor cats. If you are planning to send your cat outside, developing a strict feeding schedule can help to ensure that the kitty returns home at meal times. You can decide if once a day or twice a day is best for you. If you choose once a day, then evening feeding is usually the best solution because you want the kitty in at night and out in the day.

One potential problem that you can run into with feeding is neighbors. They may feed the kitty throughout the day or even feed her things that she prefers to what you provide. If that happens, she may simply adopt her new family. You should let your neighbors know not to feed your cat.

It is a good idea to associate feeding with a bell, whistle, or other sound. This will work as a long distance call for the kitty to return to dinner and will also be more effective than yelling and waking the neighbors (provided it is an ultrasonic or pleasant sound and not something like a gong or an air horn). The whistle will travel further than your voice, which will be useful if the kitty is lost and you are out searching.

Walking your cat on a leash is a very good way to get her used to the neighborhood and to establish boundaries. It may not work perfectly, but it certainly improves your chances of success in having the kitty stay near home if she "knows her neighborhood." It may be the case that your cat will be less inclined to roam if she is allowed to be outdoors but also gets to go on walks each day. This allows her to roam a bit while in the safety of your presence, which will reduce her desire to roam at other times. Cats are all about pleasure, so if the kitty finds it satisfying to bask in the safety of her own yard and walk only when you are around, then you will have a cat that never leaves home.

Microchips are not as expensive as you might think and can make all the difference in the world if you find that the kitty is missing for several days. Chips work better than collars for two reasons. First, collars fall off and get lost. Second, cats can injure themselves in collars, which is why most cat collars are the breakaway type. Collars are a bad idea for cats, so consider the microchip.

Once the chip is in place, there are a number of organizations that will register your contact information confidentially. Why is it important to keep your contact information confidential? Unfortunately, putting a name and address on a cat's collar has been used by criminals to rob homes in the past. They lure a pet owner to a remote location under the pretense of having found kitty while an accomplice robs the owner's house. No wonder so many people like cats more than their fellow human beings!

If you have moved to a new location and your cat was an outdoor feline in her old home, you will want to wait at least two weeks before letting her outside at her new residence. She needs time to adjust to the new surroundings and learn where her home is. The stress of the move may also cause her to act in an unusual way or attempt to run away. Finally, you will want to introduce yourselves to the neighbors.

During the kitty's indoor time, you can start engaging in behaviors that will help to ensure that she either stays in your yard or, at the very least, returns home once in a while. Chief among these preparations is feeding as mentioned above, but there are other things you can do that don't involve the kitty directly, but will have impact on her wanderings.

Neighbors

The subject of neighbors brings up an important point. Letting your cat roam the neighborhood may create problems between you and, well, everyone else. Don't assume that everyone is a cat lover or that they don't mind your cat digging in their prized rose bushes. Your cat is your responsibility and you will be liable should she cause damage. This is not to mention the fact that you probably want to be on reasonable terms with the people living near you.

You should inform your neighbors that you are trying to teach kitty to stay in her own yard and ask for their assistance. If you engage them before letting kitty out, they will appreciate your concern, be on the lookout for your cat, and know not to feed her or call animal control. Let them know that they can gently return her home if she is on their property or call you to come and claim her.

Plants

The key with cats, as said before, is to make them want to do something. If you provide an appealing outdoor place for kitty to live, she is more likely to stay home. You can start with planting cat-friendly foliage throughout your yard, then move on to repellant plants and non-plant alternatives.

These plants are not only attractive to the kitty, but they also keep fleas and ticks away. Before you plant anything in your yard, check to make sure it isn't toxic. Here is a short list of plants that cats love:

- Catnip

- Lemon grass

- Mint

- Cat grass (*Dactylis glomerata*)

- Valerian

- Wheat grass

The next step is to put plants your cat may dislike around the perimeter of your yard and anywhere else you don't want the kitty to go. This will help keep her within a perimeter, though it certainly isn't foolproof. This does not mean planting anything that will hurt the kitty, but rather planting things that she won't like. *Coleus canina* is one such plant that works on both dogs and cats. You can also plant lavender, rue, and pennyroyal to keep kitty out of certain areas.

While we are discussing plants, understand that the kitty may take a liking to your garden or your neighbor's garden. You can prepare your garden with plants as above, but that may not be enough. Consider a fence or other form of repellant to keep your furry friend away from your leafy greens.

You may also want to prepare to purchase your neighbors new plants in the event that kitty does wander. Having a little fund on the side to replace things the kitty breaks isn't a bad idea when she first starts going outside.

Plants are not the only way to go when containing the kitty. There are commercial cat repellants that may or may not work. You can also consider a fence. This is an expensive solution to keeping kitty contained but, if done right, will be highly effective.

In general, electric fences don't work for cats the way they do for dogs because cats are usually able to climb high enough to avoid a shock. If you do install a fence, you are going to have to take care to install it far enough from trees that kitty cannot jump over it and keep it in good shape. It is quite amazing just how small of a hole a determined cat can fit through.

There are ultrasonic solutions for keeping cats in (or out) of desired locations. Most work on a motion basis and send off an ultrasonic sound (humans can't hear it) when kitty moves through the beam. Cost varies dramatically on these devices and will depend on the size of your yard.

Habitat Necessities

Your cat will need an outdoor habitat that is both safe and fun. Make sure that kitty has a place where she can lay both in and out of the sun. She will also require a safe place or, preferably, several safe places that she can escape to if threatened.

The safer and happier kitty is in her own yard, the less likely she is to wander.

Some of the solutions talked about above, like foul-smelling plants and ultrasonic fences, will work quite well to keep unwanted cats from entering your yard and bothering your kitty. Neutering females is also highly recommended to keep male cats from performing courtship rituals and having massive brawls with other suitors in your backyard.

Other ways to keep unwanted cats out of your yard are to purchase a dog that is friendly with your cat but not with others, spray pheromone around the perimeter of your yard, or vigilantly spray the invading cat with water. Keeping unwanted cats away is frustrating, which is why you want to make sure your kitty does not become "that cat."

Litter Box Training

Some people believe that training a cat to use a litter box is unnecessary. However, cats do not instinctually use litter boxes and they are not "trained" by their mothers to do so. They do, however, have natural tendencies to dig, which can be exploited to get them to use the litter box. Training a kitten is far easier than training an older cat. To that end, the basics of training will be broken down into kitten and adult cat categories.

I would suggest putting a heading for "Kitten Litter Box Training here," just to keep things consistent.

You want to begin training your kitten as soon as you get it home and the best way to start is by setting up the right environment. Purchase a litter box that is large enough to accommodate your kitten once she becomes a cat but that has a low enough lip to allow her to get in while she is a kitten.

You want to select a location for the litter box that is quiet and out of the way. Cats appreciate privacy as much as we do, so respect it. It should be a location where the litter box can remain for a prolonged period of time. Moving the litter box too soon can confuse your kitten and lead to inappropriate urinating behavior.

Remember that kittens that have been living outdoors will be accustomed to digging in dirt. If you are bring a furry friend in from outside, put dirt in the litter box. You can slowly transition to litter once the cat is used to the box, but don't do so too early.

When getting started, you should expect a few accidents to occur. It is just part of having a pet and if you think of it in those terms, you will prepare ahead of time by rolling up rugs, covering furniture, and purchasing cleaning supplies. Natural cleaners are excellent for cleaning up cat urine and removing the odor. Enzymes are essential to destroying urine and its odor, so purchase a product that has enzymatic action. To cover up the odor and prevent further accidents in the same area, use a mixture of 25% white vinegar to 75% water (beware of bleaching).

Teach your kitten to use the box by placing her in it after a nap, a meal, playtime, or when she seems ready to use the bathroom. You will also want to pick her up and set her in the box after an accident. Avoid disciplining your cat just before putting her in the litter box, as she will learn to associate it with punishment. By the same token, rubbing a cat's nose in a mess or bringing her to it for a reprimand will be of little use. She will simply be confused and will start to relieve herself in hidden spots. If she does make a mess somewhere, clean it up and then put the dirty tissue in the litter box, she will then associate the box with the right place to go to the bathroom in the future.

Reward your kitten profusely for using her litter box. Use treats, love, and any other pleasant reward to let her know that she has been a good kitten. This next part may seem strange, but you should leave a small amount of urine or feces in the litter box each time you clean. Do this for the first week or two, as it will help your kitten to remember what the box is for. After the break-in period, try to keep the rest of the litter box clean by scooping it out once or twice per day. You should change the litter once per week (more often if necessary) in order to keep odor to a minimum.

Common Problems

There are a couple of problems that people commonly run into when training their kittens. By and large, problems that occur are human error and not kitten error. That is to say, if something goes wrong or the process is taking a long time, it is likely something you are doing.

The most common mistake most new cat owners make is to carry their kitten to the litter box every time. This is okay in the beginning, but your kitten will learn best if it walks to the litter box on its own. Coax your friend to the litter box with treats any time you think she might need to use the bathroom, that way she'll learn to walk over to the box by herself and won't come to you each time (a behavior you are likely to misinterpret and thus will lead to accidents).

Another common mistake is to be impatient. Even once a kitten starts using the litter box, it may have accidents. Like human children, kittens have to learn how to control their bladders and bowels and this takes time and neurologic development. Don't be upset if they have an accident here and there for the first six months or so, this is normal.

The essence of everything with cats is patience. In fact, cats are good analogies for life in that regard. Have patience with your feline companion and all will go well. The more patient you are, the stronger the bond will be between you and your cat and the closer the two of you will grow over time.

Adult Litter Box Training

There are two reasons you would need to train an adult cat to use a litter box; either the cat is newly adopted or your adult cat has stopped using the litter box. If the latter is the case, then you should be looking for either medical or behavioral issues that are the cause. Medical issues are as follows:

• Urinary Tract Infections - This is especially common in male cats. Foul odors, frequent urination, and rapid running to the litter box are all indicative of infection.

• Diabetes - Large volumes of urine, excessive drinking, and rapid changes in weight (gain or loss) are all signs of diabetes.

• Arthritis/Old age incontinence - This occurs when your cat has arthritis or some other condition, like general aging, that prevents her from reaching the litter box on time. The solution to this problem is to have more than one litter box throughout the house.

• Blocked anal glands - Indiscriminate defecation is a sign of blocked anal glands as are scooting, crying during defecations, or licking of the anal area.

• Diarrhea - This one is easy to identify.

Behavior issues that cause an otherwise well adjusted cat to stop using the litter box can be more difficult to identify. In many cases the problem will resolve on its own. Some of the more common causes include:

• A change in the type of litter you use

• The introduction of another cat

• A change in the litter box or its location in the house

• A new person in the house

In each of the cases above, time and patience are usually the solutions to determining exactly what the cause is. In many cases, it is obvious that something has triggered the behavior based on the proximity in time. In other cases, it may be more difficult.

If you are planning to switch to a different litter, you should do so gradually if possible. If you have purchased a new litter box and the cat dislikes it, you may simply need to purchase another type.

Adopting an adult cat is fantastic for both you and your new companion. The kitty gets a happy, safe, permanent home and you get a loving companion. Adopted cats are wonderful, but they bring some emotional baggage with them sometimes. Patience and love will help you work through it.

If you need to train your new adult cat to use a litter box for the first time, do so just as you would for a kitten. It is especially important to pay attention to the use of dirt rather than litter if kitty lived outdoors for a long period of time. You will probably have to experiment with different types of litter as well until you find one your cat likes. Remember that you aren't stuck with this litter since, once the kitty is using the box, you can gradually transition to another kind.

Adopted cats should have thorough medical checks. This is particularly true if they are relieving themselves in odd locations like countertops or sinks. Punishing an adopted cat is a very bad idea given that you have no way of knowing how she was treated previously. If you stir a repressed memory you could not only encourage more inappropriate bathroom behavior, you could permanently end any chance of the two of you bonding.

On rare occasions, the glue used in carpeting can have a slight ammonia smell. Your cat may mistake this for another cat marking its territory and compensate by urinating outside of the litter box. There are two ways to fix this problem. You can either put a small piece of the carpet in the litter box, reducing its size until the cat no longer urinates on the floor or you can install new carpet. Odor eliminators may work, but it is unlikely.

Behavioral issues related to urination usually resolve on their own and relatively quickly (though it probably will seem like forever). Stress is a major factor in some cat's lives when they begin urinating in inappropriate locations. It can be difficult to determine if stress is the cause, but look for other signs like pulling out fur, fear aggression, pacing, and howling. These are signs of a stressed cat. Finding the source of the stress can be difficult, but start with ruling out medical conditions. Try to provide a safe place for kitty where she can relieve some stress and relax if nothing else can be done.

Clicker Training

 Clicker training waxes and wanes in popularity among the general population, but it is an effective means of secondary reinforcement that has been used by professionals for some time. Before jumping in to how clicker training is accomplished, it is important to know how it works. This will help you to employ the technique properly and achieve optimal results.

The essence of clicker training is to associate a reward, like food, with a clicking sound so that your cat comes to understand that the clicking is an indication of good behavior and a pending reward. Clicker training is actually quite simple and can be done in about a week.

There are a number of ways in which to use clicker training. It may be especially effective when attempting to get your cat to enter its carrier, walk on a leash, ride in the car, or stop biting someone. The net result of training is that the cat understands the clicker means reward is coming and thus is happy to do whatever (for the most part) you ask of her.

Giving your cat a treat or lavishing it with praise is a form of reinforcement. Specifically, it is positive reinforcement, which means it encourages more of the behavior. Punishment is negative reinforcement because it is meant to bring about the end of a particular behavior.

Punishment does not work well; not for people and not for cats. The saying that "you catch more flies with honey" embodies the philosophy of positive reinforcement and should be something that you keep in the back of your mind when dealing with your cat. A reward is far more effective than a punishment. Any pet expert will tell you that reward and praise are the keys to training an animal to engage in a desired behavior. You will get better results at a faster rate with positive reinforcement and will not suffer the side effects (anger, shunning, etc.) that come with negative reinforcement.

Positive reinforcement can be primary or secondary. In primary reinforcement, the cat is given a reward with innate value. This may be a treat, pets, or a favorite toy. The cat wants these objects, and so giving it to her is a reward.

In secondary reinforcement, the good feelings associated with the primary reinforcement are, over time, associated with the secondary reinforcement. This is really nothing more than operant conditioning, such as was seen with Pavlov's dog. Each time the dog was fed, a bell was rung. Over time, simply ringing the bell causes the dog to salivate as much as when it saw food because it had learned to associate the bell with food. The same can be done with cats and is the basis of clicker training.

There is no special device that you need, just something that makes a sound that is audible to both you and your cat and is pleasant. Many pet stores sell clicker products, but you just need something that is unique. Some people use a click of their tongue in order to keep their hands free while others use a handheld clicker. The choice is yours.

Clicker training can be performed by following the six steps here. If you do this for 10 minutes per day, your cat will learn simple tricks inside of two weeks and then you'll be ready to go for more complicated lessons. For this to work, you'll need to have an abundant supply of treats that your cat absolutely loves. In the example, getting the cat to follow a stick will be the goal, but anything can be substituted.

The goal of the clicker is to use it as a secondary feedback mechanism so that your cat knows she is on the right track for a reward. Note that a reward always comes at the end of a series of clicks. Clicking without the reward at the end will extinguish (bring an end to) the behavior eventually and you will have to start over with training.

Step 1

Click and give your cat a treat. Wait until she is done eating and looks back up then do the same thing again. This first step is all about associating the sound of the click with the treat so that your cat learns that the click is a positive sound and associates it with good feelings. This step is sometimes referred to as "loading the clicker" and it must be done in the order (1) click and then (2) treat.

Step 2

The next step is to get the cat to follow a target or engage in some appropriate behavior. In the case of getting the cat to follow a stick, place the stick close to the cat and as soon as she moves toward it, sound the click and provide a treat. Click while the behavior is happening and not before or after. Note that the click comes before the treat.

Step 3

You can start moving the target (or stick) now and getting kitty to engage in more complex behavior (run-up ramps, jump, etc.). Your goal will be to have her make two or a few steps (walk and turn for example) before the reward. You will click with each correct step, but hold the reward until a serious of two or three steps (with clicks) are complete.

Step 4

Start adding verbal commands to the mix at this point. When your cat gets the sequence right and responds to the verbal command, sound the click. You want to sound the click at each correct move. For instance, if the cat is to sit up and then paw the stick, you sound the click when she sits and again when she paws the stick. Only at the end do you reward her.

Step 5

The routine is now engrained in the cat's mind, so you may not need the clicker any longer. You can try getting the kitty to go through the whole routine without the clicker and then reward her at the end. Return to the clicker any time you need to reinforce part of the behavior.

Quick Tips

1. Equality

Get down on the same level with your cat. This creates a congenial atmosphere where the two of you are equals working toward the same goal.

2. Food Talks

Hungry cats are more easily trained. A cat with a full stomach will not be interested in treats, so use small bits. Smaller treats can be finished faster, which means that training will proceed faster. Use only one treat each time (except at the end).

3. Time is of the Essence

Keep early sessions short. Twenty clicks should be the maximum when you are first starting.

4. Keep it Happy

Keep sessions pleasant. Cats don't tolerate punishment and will simply refuse to participate.

5. Two's a Crowd

If you are attempting to train two cats, start by training one at a time. Move on to two only when they each have their own routine down.

6. Patience

Be patient. This should be fun for you and your cat. If it is not fun, you should reconsider.

7. Picky Eater

On rare occasion, a cat will not respond to treats. If you kitty doesn't like treats, simply substitute with something she does like such as a favorite toy or a scratch behind the ears.

8. The Human Element

Failures in training are usually a result of slow rewards or inappropriate delays. This is particularly true of aggressive cats, which require rewards to follow promptly.

Cat Training FAQ

It's not uncommon for cat owners to experience bizarre behavior from their cats. One second cats are behaving normally and the next they are  running around the house at full speed making weird noises.

It is in a cat's nature to respond to their senses - whether it is real or perceived. Sometimes, their advanced senses can detect things that are not perceived by humans. When this happens, the best thing is to move the cat to a quiet area in your home and speak in a soothing way until they calm down. Try to limit the amount of space in the house they have access to. They will soon understand they are in no danger.

Question: We own several cats and one of them is harassing all the others. It is very aggressive and often, the other cats will not eat or drink when this cat is around. I love and want to keep all of my cats but I would like them too get along. What can I do?

While dogs usually adopt these sorts of pack-like behaviors, it is not uncommon for cats to assume roles within a social grouping. Some cats may consider themselves leaders and adopt an aggressive attitude towards the rest of the pack.

The leader will become so territorial and protective of their food and water, to the point of attacking other cats when they approach. The best solution is to separate the aggressive cat from the others. Do not feed them all together and have their food dishes in separate rooms. After they've eaten, remove the dishes so that there is no temptation. This can help calm the cats and prevent even bigger problems.

Regarding territorial issues, you should keep an eye on the cats when they are together, once you feel the situation is getting tense, remove the bullying cat from the area. This allows the cat to know you are the dominant force in the house and that the area does not belong to them.

Question: Recently my cat has been meowing nonstop and I don't know why. What should I do?

Firstly, be sure that there is no reason for your cat meowing. Check the cat carefully to see if there is anything medically wrong. Look at your cat's whole body, checking ears, eyes, teeth and claws. Look for signs of infection or if they express discomfort when you touch any areas. If you're unsure, have your cat checked by a veterinarian.

If there are no physical problems, meowing and noises are usually for attention seeking. They meow when they want you to pet them, play with them, feed them or let them outside. If it is to seek attention, and you feel it is excessive, do not reward them by answering all them all every time they meow. Leave them alone in a room, they will eventually get bored, and over time will learn that they won't get special attention every time they meow or make noises.

Question: My cat is overly active at night. He begins running all over the place, making noises and knocking things down on the floor, ultimately waking me up. How can I stop that?

Cats are crepuscular, meaning they are most active during dusk and dawn hours. There is nothing you can do to prevent this since cats do not have a circadian rhythm like humans. Instead, try to keep the cat entertained during these hours while you sleep.

Scatter toys in the places your cat roams, and make sure there's a clean litter tray and a water dish. You can also play with the cat right before you sleep so it uses some of its energy. If your cat is still noisy, try confining it into a room further away from you or get some earplugs. Cats are nocturnal animals, and you must find a solution so that their activities won't bother you while you sleep.

Question: My cat keeps stealing human food whenever it gets an opportunity. It happens even in our presence. How can we teach them they're not allowed to eat human food?

Cats follow their instinct, and training them to not eat the tempting food in front of them is almost impossible. What you can do is give a quick response whenever that happens: clap your hands and say "no" in a firm and powerful voice. Then remove the cat from the room. The cats should be well fed before you sit down to eat, so feed them about half an hour beforehand. Also, you can keep the cat out of the room when there is food around. It's hard to make cats go against their instincts, but these measures should reduce the frequency of food theft.

Question: Can my old cat(s) still be trained?

Absolutely. Although cats are most responsive and eager to learn at a young age, they can keep doing so throughout their life. You just need to have more patience once they reach adulthood but it can certainly be done. Age is less of a factor than it may seem, as even old cats receiving training for the first time have proven to be able to learn new things. Health is much more important than age, as sick or injured cats will have trouble focusing on what you are trying to teach it. A good training program can instill habits and behaviors that are beneficial both to you and your cat so it is never too late to consider it.

Final Words

It has been said before, but it warrants repeating. Patience is a virtue when training your cat, so take your time and enjoy what you are doing. Cats are very receptive to your tension level, so don't attempt training when you are upset or overly tense. Take your time and both you and your kitty will be happy.

Cats are wonderful companions and will be faithful, loving friends for their entire lives if you treat them with respect. Like humans, each cat has a personality that is all its own. Some cats are calm and reserved while other cats are wild and adventurous.

If you are selecting a kitten, you can determine its personality by the way it greets you. A calm, affectionate cat will come over readily and seek attention. It will be at least as interested in you as it is in the other kittens in its litter. More independent cats will likely play with the others, bolt from one activity to the next, and generally spend less time with you than they do with their own tails. Neither choice is right or wrong; you simply must decide for yourself which personality type suits yours.

As a very rough generalization, males tend to be more affectionate than females and calmer as well. This is particularly true of neutered males. This is a rough rule, however, as many female cats are perfectly friendly. Females tend to wander less when outdoors.

When you are assessing a cat for personality, pick her up, rub her ear, and touch her paws and tail. Some cats will find these activities pleasant and others will find them highly irritating. The cat that finds these irritating is likely to be less affectionate and more independent. If you happen to find a cat that enjoys being upside down (not that you should flip them over, but they may do it themselves), then you have an easy-going feline on your hands.

It is an interesting observation, and may not be entirely true, but many veterinarians and cat owners claim that tortoise shell and calico cats are higher strung and "quirkier" than other cats. There is no scientific basis for this, but it does have strong anecdotal backing. Of course, it may be no different than black cat superstition, but it is worth considering if you are choosing one cat from a group.

The bottom line with any cat is patience. You must seek first to understand and then to be understood. Try to put yourself in your cat's shoes (or litter box - but not literally) when things aren't going smoothly. This is the best way to understand what is bugging your friend and bring about a resolution. The more understanding you are of your cat, the more understanding she will be of you. Your relationship with your furry feline companion is no different than that with a human (sans communication). There is a give and take. Compromise will lead to a richer, fuller life for the both of you.

Pamela

Free Gift

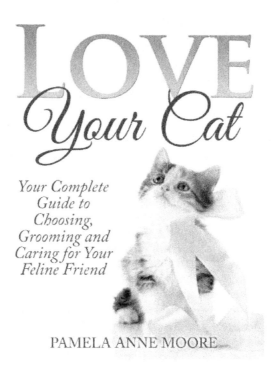

I am a great believer in delivering extra value whenever I get the chance, and so I have decided to give you one of my other best-selling titles "Love Your Cat" free of charge as a thank you for buying this book.

To download your free book and sign up to your free 'Caring for Your Feline Friend' newsletter, just copy the link into your browser and enter the e-mail address you would like your free book and newsletter sending to.

bit.ly/1lRfZYQ

One Last Thing

Thank you for buying 'Cat Training is Easy!' I hope that you enjoyed it and now have the confidence that with the right instructions, persistence and a little bit of patience training your cat really is possible.

If you liked this book it would be a big favor to me if you could leave an honest review at Amazon or Goodreads. Thank you.

Pamela

CPSIA information can be obtained
at www.ICGtesting.com
Printed in the USA
LVOW13s2114191216
518019LV00014B/992/P